Mirror Magic

T0308035

Mirror Magic

John Sakkis

ROOF BOOKS
NEW YORK

ISBN: 978-1-931824-92-7
Library of Congress Control Number: 2020947169

Cover artwork: Contrail (Three Views) by Joel Gregory.
Copyright © Joel Gregory, 2020.

Author's photo: Stian Rasmussen

Acknowledgments: Selections from *Mirror Magic* were published in
the group reading chapbook *Confluence* (Aggregate Space Gallery), as
a broadside from Nomadic Ground Coffee, in SFAQ#5, New American
Writing #33, AMERARCANA #5, and *The Emerald Tablet* anthology,
thanks to the editors.

for Monica and Constantine

 This project is supported, in part, by an award from
the National Endowment for the Arts.

 This book is made possible, in part, by the New York
State Council on the Arts with the support of Governor
Andrew Cuomo and the New York State Legislature.

Roof Books
are published by
Segue Foundation
300 Bowery, New York, NY 10012
seguefoundation.com

Roof Books
are distributed by
Small Press Distribution
1341 Seventh Street
Berkeley, CA. 94710-1403
800-869-7553 or spdbooks.org

Table of Contents

CAP. KIRK
THE PRIME
      DIRECTIVE
TO WORSHIP
NEPTUNE LEAPING
AND LINGERING
PROGRESSIVE
HOUSE/ IT BELONGS
TO THE DEAD
ALTERNATE EARTH
ROMAN INSURGENT
XENOMORPH

The Emerald Tablet

There is a tract that says break the stone if you drop it
twice
Though no animal miracles were effected upon consideration
There is an oil from the outset that seeps silly offspring
The way a wind surfer rides white water, the freeway in front
Peeling shoulders a human container set back as an obstacle to
leap over

Please excuse this circle of constellations, the quad is where
We gain the weight of precious stones on top of all that other
Sperm and tincture, naturally you'll be offered a job outside
The alembic after bowling in the Presidio where wind blown
Trees act as one animal naturally watery and oily seeping from
Their weekend gaze moving about your bowels

The earth is its nurse so says the sucker free City on a mad dash
Through food assimilated in my body as iron and calories
Are discarded as a wonderful juice though sometimes bare
and dry
As a summer day fondling my talisman on a skateboard in circles
And circles never marking these patterns on feet indelible
and religious
The way wheels are runes carving out a language in clouds
the best
Lines are burning and roasting an alembic weather this weekend
We'll see roasting and calcinations, the black pitchy matter
moving
Here and there, this and that in veins and drops the blacktop flat
And undulating in groups of offspring carving out a language
that's
A real language read and skinned bursting horizontal in little
slices

That resemble cursive puffs dissipating in glossy eyes through
a screen
On the hillside crawling with creatures invisible as a water
spider in
The morning light multiplied tenfold for coloration

This way is traversed by the sages, such a simple solution
When the power increases this speedy distillation bends its knees
I have no change on the Lake, I'm running cold and stiff
Whichever mile marker we manifest we cheat by degrees
That the weather is warm and salty, that this solar power
Is a Greek word, running on the back at times crass and smelly
Many different minerals find their function when fingered
Though it helps to be traveling state-side, or at least
Leaving whichever state you were born in to get at the ferment
Festering a passive "materia," then fall down and fall further
And what a gnomic cliché the earth as our nurse but don't worry
About assimilation, food fortifies the occasion whether bare
or dry
A bifurcated mammal talks mammalian words when spoken to
Roasted on the spit and non fixed and fluent using the word
"spirit"
Thoroughly and clearly is a virtue at the base on the naval
descending
Through substances neither here nor there though suffocating
Yourself while an alchemical animal you'll retain some kind of
Phantom memory while repeating "spirit, spirit, spirit"
Crossing state lines with a particular disposition and noble
humor

There are myriad steps to consider before transitioning into a MINERAL MONSTER

Step 1- Instant Travel Shift

Get out of human skin then wonder what it would look like to enter PARADISE.

Step 2- Energy Shift

Highlight the transcendent moments of your day by illustrating on paper all the erogenous zones of your body from least sensitive to most sensitive. Treat the paper and pencil as you would the genitalia of a trusted partner, project yourself into her body from every cardinal point. Feel yourself growing lighter and brighter and buzzing with energy. Repeat the command, "make me a MINERAL MONSTER."

Step 3- Flight Shift

Hover as long as you can in your bedroom, aiming midway between your dresser and the ceiling, extend your arms so that your fingernails begin to tingle and itch. Center yourself so that your balls begin to rotate and swell. Imagine yourself shooting into the ceiling at hyperspeed.

Step 4- Virtual Reality Shift

Walk into a mirror, movie, TV, or computer screen. Avoid gazing into your own eyes as this will cause an unshakeable sense of dread. Add commands for shifting into specific minerals, e.g., "make me an Amber giant, a Malachite giant" etc. etc.

Step 5- Melting Hands Shift

Look at your hands and watch them melt, then look away. Repeat this a few dozen times. If you have bedroom eyes you will have a hard time accepting this. This will cause a transmogrification of the body, shifting you into the mineral realms. Add commands for a more desirable body type, e.g., "take me to the moon."

Step 6- Spin Shift

Spin around as fast as you can until you vomit.

Step 7- Falling Shift

Step backwards off a concrete sidewalk while pressing the tip of your tongue to the roof of your mouth. The phenomena associated with tonguing the contours of your mouth can be useful during MINERAL MONSTER transition. The falling backwards sensation can be disorienting and scary, do not panic, your flesh and bone are merely ascending into a higher state of consciousness. Do not cross your legs and do not speak while experiencing these phenomena. Continue body exercise for two minutes or until emerging as a MINERAL.

Let's make a plan
Next time we hit the lake later
Let's take note of our knots
But all our girlfriends call any muscle
Tension kneaded a kinky time warp
Any which way you swing the bat
The fluid leaks into a medium trance
I want to say that taking off my shirt
Is political, but I've felt a boxing mania
Down, down, down on my shoulders
The lake is not shit, it is a manmade dissociation
But not poisonous, there is a heavy flow over the water
A slick skim and slight falling sensation
That's the power of distillation during the warmer months

The lake is constantly "lake-like"
I won't swim concealed in reflexes
Feeding on any microorganism in my wake
All sustenance must vanish of course
Into my webbed fingers stiff with muck
Inhaling those tainted spores as the pregnant
Fish I am, a perfect geometry of snowflakes
Takes the easy route shedding flakes by design
Raising the water by my gross lake-like body

The drive home is a feeding frenzy
We should all flee from it

Range Rover to bright
brain poundage paper
though turntables be othered
on the scale of your breath control
I tic toc my minutes
NIMBY pansies get butterflies
"shadow pollution" kills birds
so rents go up and over
you laugh at the needles
that stick to your meddling
white picket fences painted
brown nosed babies
you seem so fascinated
we called it in from here
to there, hear her cowboy boots
drag while her fingers run
the lines of her underwear
the course is clear, do nothing,
resist, inspect your betters
newer and never
prepare your vacation, leave
California to the birds
no anemone can walk the earth
with false confidence
from word
to thing on the freeway,
scorched in summer
and baked
throughout the day
lunchtime is most visible
in its insistence
big time moxie proven
by sports talk radio, fasting

is only a parting of ways
expunging the cellular
creatures go down on you
en masse, with runner's legs
the ligature of pay day
sews The Nightingale
frightened
overstaying his welcome

Please leave
this sweet light
and render me
phosphorescent tubeway splatter genome
the Saints, three-faced
I summon you
in sub-zero climes
I skip rocks on Sunday
aiming for a tree
the size of a horse
it's bark yields *euphoria* when hit,

the rule is
flee down the stairs
into the street
with mud on your face,
flee constipated
cleaving the air

This is how I quest
play in the rain
phosphorescent train wreck
the reason why
my friends hoax is varied
sometimes they obviate
the buddy system
causing widespread panic
they mettle out
pain in increments, do you hear me?
so much activism, so much
splatter guts through the bullhorn
because midway along life's journey
marriage is an allegory
subduer becomes subdued
not exactly a subtle allegory,
do you hear the metamorphic
flashbang grenades a' bursting
the pigs poisoned blood
is bursting with good intentions
I can't stand this rain in August
and then I lay down, large and small

This is a "factual" text
the same committee preceding
and leap frogging along the banks
of the hanky panky bears the weight
of all that bullish rigmarole
as so often in the history
of therapeutics
a serendipitous thing happened on the way to supper
we got game and came correct
this is a power trip
without treachery
come Lord, become
reincarnated, undeterred
and unfettered
"the millennium" is a confusing term
and you are a headless oracle mumbling
'this generation shall not pass
directly or indirectly
into the abyss'
not to exaggerate too much
but I'm betting on it: copious kisses,
allusions and legends,
PRIDE wears a scepter and crown

An eel has teeth like fish bones
an eel has watery gray teeth
like the redwoods that
over time
turn to stone
I was told
to beware the surface of the river
I logged a complaint

the Eel River reeks,
the true point
of this hike
is of no consequence
there is no infection,
we throw rocks
at the water that hovers
if you can hit this hovering mass
space itself bounds forth
rocks hover when handled
no longer
in neutral
space

Virgula Divina

a common tune
on an Autumn evening
to hear it is Byzantine
follow the croaking toads along the river
into the woods
you call it nature, that ever collapsing
incertitude, joy to the herald of geese
honking, the lake to the North
in arousal, a new season
in heaven and proud
of the bruises you accrue
gripping the slick sticks between
your fingers, someone is waving their arms
and running at the geese, the
dark water of Autumn
you can smell it, that sour stench,
the animals are lucid in bursts
of eye contact, while the geese
keep cold above the river
this water, this drawn-out
Y-shaped ravine

Knead the bread
whose biology is sour and fatty
I forget if it's the Eastern Span who
rose on the third day,
in this way, according to the scriptures
nomenclature is a silly thing
beating my fingers against
the irreparable
havoc you reap
I open the bedroom window, there's no
fog anymore, or wind, just the seeds
feeding the weight of this spectacle
there isn't any time at all
the irreparable thing you've become
stuck without suspicion
without separation, the will
no longer reveals anything
other than what you already know
the will is ridiculous
the very fact that one even speaks
rising early in the morning
kissing the icon
repeatedly

Dumb Daemonic

Sunday Doctor/ you are better clothed than I am/

drink hella water
I don't know nothin' about Grizzly Peak
you know, Berkeley Hills?/ above the carousel
naming names at that mangy moody lake
there's nothing better than a frozen doughnut
watch your step out here/
for all penitent men shall pass
these treacherous roads less traveled
strong medicine, juju, on the choo choo train
waving goodbye, it's football season

Hardbacksides Custer
under Obamacare
oh Grandfathered in
oh great one, members
of the Ensemble encore
the deductible is less
yes, but it's unaffordable,
this stuff isn't fixable
SF is uber yay or nay
no room for the middle
pursuing Col. who on horseback

I too feel amphibious
dumb daemonic
like a frog expanding horizontally
the way men's faces expand as they age
you better have a resolution prepped
and ready to rock, like shooting fish
in a barrel, guilt gets easier
miles get harder and longer
sleep gets got
and ambition gets complicated,
I don't want to run a restaurant
I get that squishy feeling in my belly
before bedtime
I think of the tadpoles
rotting between my fingers
their skin sticking to my skin
and I feel like nothing matters more
than patting myself on the back
for all the great content
I consume

I'm done making my kid's childhood magical
the animals are leaving Yellowstone
immediately, immediately
the girls are naked and they dance
the Ancient Greek
do the Rustic Cow, do that dance you do
rise up dim-sighted girls, don't front, you're bringing the
Dawn
and you know it, bring it correct
and hurry up with it, these portraits
are cracking me up
these portraits changed the way I saw animals

That cherry pit
the width of the lamplight
rations of water
washed down with
the fruit, the sea
all over me
where material runs deep
nary a reply, nobody sees the
fishing net at night
the large mermaids in my mind
nodding off, a thong
leotard misremembered
at the bluff
a place to sit
high above the water mark

Tuesday night's earthquake
gobbled me up
mouth to mouth
at my bedroom window
making my own oceans
and the repetition
of the drowned
I used to think I was fat
until floating
nothing's funny,
taste level is a real thing
please taste this water,
my cousins say Contra Costa
is saltier than the sea
show me a plant and water
quickly, quickly
I'd rather skim the surface
then put my shoulders into it
this floating earth on the surf
so much dissipation
as we sleep in the backseat
shedding salt, trading shapes
in common with this light
going from white to white
watching the earth undulate
and the cars gone crazy
floating and falling
and floating

Battlestar/ Brittle Star
knock on wood to say hey
consider parking further away
this fungus growing out of my tooth
the joyous mammary memories
of a trip to the supermarket
I'm so sick of Indian Summer
Brittle you, the little stunner
a jubilant fly on the wall
I'm scared of Daylight Savings too,
there is no future so we may as well turn back
the roving animals in charge
it's a ghost of a day
battle me/ Battle you

Phenomena

Let's start with the premise
we worship you,
the telepathic insects of Italy
eating the shit of shining mortals,
that nightgowns may hint at cobwebs
is obvious enough
this metaphor in Virgo
a needle and yarn unraveling The Coprophage,
an adolescent mind
plucked
from dead hands
teenage girls are diabolical
I guess
the Great Sarcophagus
is small and poisonous,
it's ESP is fleshy and parasitic,
teenage girls make the greatest detectives the world has ever
known:
listen carefully to girlish intuition
avoid vertebrate carcasses

If I paint my face
with egg yolk and vinegar
am I being melodramatic,
if you say you prefer liquid beeswax
I may spasm an insect
from the center of my forehead,
if you would only stop fighting
the subject matter
you might realize
those things in your bedroom
are just charnel
there
for the talking

I seek to attend
to all my leaky emulsions
by bitter necessity
and hour by hour
my Agamemnon face
turns to 7 colors of gold
a binding turpitude gone apostolic
so now I'm the man
with the golden arm
my garments smeared with olive oil
my turntable adorned with golden tassels,
I box women and children frequently
and make love to myself
once a week
eventually I'll be housed
in a church
with other weepy schematics
eventually I'll become
the gray misty North
I've always felt myself to be

Nike+

Just WAXWORK if you want to WAXWORK 2, nobody cares
a "fun bag" is a testicle
and the buffalo
owes his extermination
very largely to his own unparalleled stupidity
I miss the smell of Gundam
beyond the village
your smile makes flowers grow
and your tits make them bloom
this horse-drawn surrey, this massive Dutch windmill
flying overhead
seems pretty rational to worship the sun
to replace the word "skateboard"
with the word "Abraham Lincoln"
every time it appears
in Thrasher Magazine
from the palm lined BLVDs
breakin' bread with my Papa/
breakin' bread
breakin' bread with my Mama
behind the arcade, blood orange
and Starburst on a promontory
seeds stuck in my teeth
salt peanuts salt peanuts
I'm hemorrhaging fans
as fast as my bikini body
my hands are melting
along the meandering backroads
the soft bigotry of Soft Surrealism
these jewel like coves,
these soft little dapper doves
perched on my windowsill
I have legs that won't quit
just hit it and split it

tis' very fresh, my updo
pardon the rumor please
a very petite rumor
the kind where we find
a Pavilion of Poets among
"crumbly ear wax"
like sea grass,
mermaids swim, Native Americans
ride horses
and a Spanish galleon
sails across the sea
what silly entropy among
other cretinous abnormalities,
unfairly it's an unruly bunch
reminiscent of an early
western landscape
complete with a covered bridge
it's a synesthesia thing
I summon you
that thing you do, that handshake
baby's on fire and we're glowing
like metal
do you like the taste of blood,
do you like driving the solid-hoofed horses
through the ditch?

I hate the way I signify

poseurs look like flowers
blooming ashes in round puffs/

she's a straight shooter
corpuscular, marriageable

I plied him with gold
and he laughed in my face

I wet my palate with horror comics
a big peach pit of a fantasy

so many friends on their little jaunts
tickling the balls
at the back of my brain
there is a rapping on the wall
bewitching my REM
I enjoy adult company, I enjoy bedtime

America is pretty cool
lame-ass teleporting zombies
the immiscible populations of
mouth froth, Ave Maria
or breakfast beer
I always accidentally end up in Alameda
in the apple orchard
the island of Tyre was my nurse
my emergencies
preclude the news
what is this little lamb doing here
the wonderful Witch Tree
my doctor falling smack dab
on her Fire Season, the olive oil
in my throat lubes a testosterone effect
this beautiful beer on Sunday morning
I recently read about
the Miracle Tomato of Bradford
which depicts a story
where Ave Maria
kills every superhero
and supervillain
in the Marvel Universe
including
herself
ten thousand eggs are hidden in my pockets
the way to vaporize a new generation
is to lie with the scarecrow
who wanders lazily among sycamores
my heritage is very much alive
among these ever-expanding
carpets of vineyards
the miracle of four-wheel drive

when you work 8 hrs a day
my doctor told me
to visit more historical sites
that can be enjoyed
in a more garrulous way

Trauma is arousing when revisited
there is a danger
of getting stuck in the mud
but the dunes
look like watercolor paintings,
fossilized seashells,
my gaping maw
this straw man argument
is a confusing day trip
to the beach
the theme was tongue
I'm more annoyed than anything/
the way I mourn
is a sadistic whiplash
there are cats clawing at my arms
in this one location
on the entire planet

My druthers are filthy
nipples cracked from running
burrs in my socks
from frolicking so much
Merry Super Bowl
a spectre
soars believably
above the Kaiser building
I don't believe women
shower as much as men
I apologize,
where is the bathroom?
this pus is putrid and white
this healing putrid blood
of Hades
like a string of pearls
posted up
at Fairyland
I just ran 5.72 mi with Nike+

**BARONESS
ELSA VON
FREYTAG-
LORINGHOVEN
DEVIL
WORSHIP
FROM
CODPIECES
TO CORSETS
FIND THE FACTS
INSTANTLY**

Duck Duck Goose
don't worry about it
it's okay in the morning
to say you slept like a rock
just don't Daisy In The Dell
don't don't don't DUCK DUCK
Razzle Dazzle oyster pirates
your mounting dread okay?
just reread the article titled
I Wrote A Letter To My Mother
at Jack London Square, no no
no, nope Duck Duck Splash
Duck Duck Animal

The Massacre at Sand Creek
I don't park there anymore
because I need to sleep
watch rations/ give us thy meat
in economic terms
whores aren't semantic/ and words
are war and words are war
meant sweetly/ The Chapel
Of Chimes greets me at the door
I scalp hurriedly and feign furious

I don't care about the weather
and he was Good
a lodestone
the leading stone
more well-balanced shamanistic claptrap
when it comes to getting naked
when it comes down to instigating the aircraft
these edible white women
lookiloos in orbit
and he was Good
in Fishtown, PA
when I say "don't shit me"
just keep drinking water and shut up
hella malaprops
I shit you not
I'm a bubble wrap B-Boy, smell smell smell
say that's really swell Mr.
say you're a bottom dweller skimming Cul de Sac
clean, like a mean Reaper you give good BONE
let's play kick the can down the road/ TELEPHONE
repeat after me "my bloody gums receding"
"my buddy knows no bleeding"
"my buddy's nose knows no's"
and I really couldn't remember
your text preference whether
your auto-didact was fuzzy
and x-rated but yes, definitely
human and stiff as a stream
straightening out small tweak-
ers huffing and puffing above
me working the floor
till kingdom come
[starts couplets]

Sparks Outrage on the internet
[starts couplets]
the Bonnie Bay Bridge of Autumn
the screaming meemies gave us the heebie-jeebies
living ghosts go down the logger's trail

chewing cud at the crossroads,
Vanishing Hitchhikers never get where they're going

Honey in the horn
no way to tell where we're going
though the baubles be shining a thick pesticide
how do you pronounce asystole
in this deranged
comeuppance
what does the title Mouth to Mouth evoke
as an uncorrupted youth,
OMG gimme a break
the human race
can be tampered with
Marble Madness is notoriously impossible
I just ran 4.22 mi with Nike+
vainglorious in my evil ways
I blame the lookiloos for my illness, this
self-trance, this hypnosis due
to sensory deprivation
the concurrent drone of
consecutive failure
my face is swollen
I meant sweetheart not sweetmeats
I gave myself a black eye
it's so fun to be a part of
this feeding frenzy

have you ever kissed someone so deeply you gave yourself a black eye?

return to asking questions when rising in the morning

can you conjure a fig

make light of aggressive platitudes

skateboard an elementary school in your dreams

I've landed everything I've attempted

I'm waking up drenched in sweat reaching for the horse saddle

the difference between secretion and excretion is table manners

the tunnel under the world
swollen and pagan
I was highly disappointed
Holy Father
who steals his bread
holy sycophant skating
on Instagram
swimming then floating
then playing house
fishing for crawdads with
bologna and bread
in the deep end
like an imaginary tree
rising 104 feet,
as I dream again
of this house's cold currents

I notice this house is secluded
its currents, streams,
roots meander
I choke on it
like long fingernails tickling
between my legs
no *corpus delicti* laughing at the depth
of this leafy harbor
just an overly forensic attitude
to parse this fertile ground
to notice how books
speak to each other
how hungry they make us

Bedeviled and bedazzled
stuffed animals
nautical me on the jovial sea
holy fuckamole
ear flush me to paradise
ordinary husks
left to dry in the sun
which blond ass do you prefer?
help me, hold me
please hecka hover above me
get off my chest
you horrible hag
sorry I'm a little creamy
in the pride of morning
in the hurry-skurry
a time-lapse short subtitled
"For Some Reason Sleeping On Your Back Leaves You More
Prone To Attack"

I forgot to curate my bed this morning
serendipity loves company
running up my legs
in the middle of the night
I go walking in my sleep
from the mountains of faith
to a river so deep
and limp dicking
first thing in the morn
your lips, the color of an under-ripe pear
I've always enjoyed
xtreme compartmentalization
these persimmons smell so horny
a solipsistic somnambulance
that conjures
the living and dead
the bountiful fruit
in your ears, the eroticism of panic
you know this
but keep doing what you've done
this pretty predictable dumb-show
I'm trembling and walking to my car
I just ran 4.41 mi with Nike+

"White," "Gold" and "Green"
our names are revealed
like a suit of cards,
I thought I recognized
a leap year and blushed red
I would note here
only children are ill-prepared
for fire, that a lampshade
made of onion-skin
makes a deep broth
that the ocean is filled with waxpaper
and animals,
if I could live in insomnia
I would be truly asserted
as two natures
nevertheless
I'm using both my right and left hands

(April)

I dreamt of the
Lodestone,
Aceyalone
those blue belly lizards
those cretinous thugs
lover of loving can be about so much:
meditation, dieting, the loving is
like metal in the mouth
that move where
my Mom, she makes trains
I should have been an athlete
with a temperament,
all of these words rotate
do you like the taste of blood?
like metal
in the mouth
a robust
and healthy sexuality

"fuck the canon" shouted the Barbarians
#cancel your banners
bar, bar
Happy 4th!
I just slept for 12 hours

Venus is a kind of hell
I really like her freckles though,
like tiny temper tantrums, unripe olives,
like small islands
her oceans were formed without
any help from life, the earth
is a barren wasteland
awkwardly whispering to the wind
"I want to put my mouth
on your mouth"

Snake

in a dream
I'm foraging
for edible yellow flowers
I'm wishing that we stopped
to place a marker
not knowing what was edible
or not
pacing as I saw you
dog-faced, baboon
it's my fault
my body
impressing this
nocturnal symbolism
but wavering
with half dried figs
in my mouth

I just ran 2.99 mi with Nike+
MY FACE IS BIGGER THAN MY NACHOS
without the fog out here
it's harder to love and elope,
I'm dragging this tender soil
with the tips of my fingers
counting one
Shadrach, 2 Meshach and 3 Abednego
do I have mono or euphoria
I eat like an old man
it must be/
the plutonium in me
I'm growing tired of being alone
in this Rendlesham Forest Incident,
Loup Garou is hungry
for want of Spring, I'm suffering
an engorged antibiotic emergency
knowing full well
that I suffer
from severe
nostalgia

My beautiful girlfriend
demure as a tortoise shell,
the Rustic Cows are roving
and mad in Ancient Greece
so many odes to ruddy tattoos
on the brink of a b-boy battle
so many cows between her fingers
a healthy aggression regardless
of whatever kind of DAWN
shows up in the story
the name of a crown with rustic…
no not a rustic, but ruddy rather
a ruddy ornamental privilege
is called a diadem, and I saw
King Philip's weathered diadem
encased in a glass display,
his face imprinted on the tomb
men have died there as we descend
and squat, don't say a surfeit of gambling
say gaffled and soaring
over the three fingers of the peninsula
scolded drunk in a swimming pool
with navigation through the χωριό
we steered
towards big rocks
to be flayed in the sun
two big skewers soaked in seawater
holding our hides towards HEAVEN
a hecatomb of honey
everyday drifting with seafaring grace
a substantial home away from home
this wreck that the DAWN brings
at this point in the plot

Two bodies can become foliage
if neither has a name
that awkward metamorphosis into
the third person,
or perhaps it's a kind of syntax
that the bread levitates
after being blessed
we prepare meaning
behind this hunger,
I was told that this bread
isn't holy until resonances
take hold O namesake
oh father Bull intercede
with this fasting
your namesake
overlooks and harangues
the garden which is 2 blocks
from my conducting
oh please
this tree in bloom
this elevated language
burgeoning an allowance
of acknowledging
that yes, this is fire
this is a plum tree
you know by name
deep purple rotting
here I shape this garden
and the blood in my ear
is just a phase speaking
again and in thrall
and again
I call by name

in bloom you adorn me
St. Basil

Coyote

I used to ride horses
and snack on pomegranates

I have blood on my sleeve
because I cut my hand

another sea-monster
lured from Greece

the thicket of the devil
as a magnet, Laughing Mountain

do not answer me

The bags are better since the ban
bueno? oh boy I'm falling asleep,
I didn't know
the CAPRIOTE hung in the corner,
what a scaredy-cat creep
my arms are bouncing out of my arms,
every time he lurches forward
I'm skywriting, fingering the air
CAPRIOTE IS A PUSSY
come and get me big boi
I want to project!
take me to the ceiling!
where is that rope,
climb the rope!
my body is an aggressive
shit talker, I have no control
of the fear I fear, I'm definitely
a dumb defensive animal,
I'm not sure if these are
my familiars
or if the menagerie
is being cat called
when I close my eyes

VEGAS!

I've been to Wyoming on holiday
Big Sky, USA
it seems to me
that UFOs are on fire
the Holy Books' aflame,
as the crab said
when he got the snake
in his claw
'form is alive'

the desert is a necromancer
the songs of children
flare like flame

I wish I had white eyelashes
and a pink lemonade
a pierced tragus
and the collapse of the internet

I guess I should listen
to Black Sabbath now

exhaustion
demands
an active astonishment
like 'the desert is dead, I come from the desert'
nobody knows what sorrow I've seen
slobber
I vacationed in Mediterrania
the food was just wonderful

Spill a whiskey
your Jason mask is ready
at the river a water tick bit my belly
there is no HEAVEN, only bread
you are one of them that eats their GOD
only folly, I'm praying not to doze
during the drive home, I'm feeling frisky
static RADIO and Redwoods
let's download the rest and get busy,
I'll visit when I'm ready
Lodge-Builder, Sun Dancer, Fire-Fighter
what tools will you get for Christmas?
I bet a sailboat and tackle, a new LOVE
you'll do fine
cowboy up,
every year is the same
fool's gold for a fire sign, water is my woman
this conjuring stick in the mud,
this New Year's Eve resolution
stop squatting for a second and jam out
like the flower-loving-honey-bee does

Invective Poetry
was not actually
expected to kill
its victims

Vinegar will dissolve limestone,
Honeydew,
Rasputin's Dick,

Geoduck,
Al Alburquerque,

Chlayms
Bysshe pleez...

I just ran 4.41 mi with Nike+
one vote, one facia
degustibus non disputandum est...

I woke up with a clove of garlic in my vagina/
all [ancient] Greek bogies are female
rain boots are always good in summer
stunner/
stunner/
stunner/

the encomium explodes
by way
of text bubbles
into three fleshy
cigarette
burns the sacred
putrefaction
the scarification
below the wrist
figures fool's
gold figures
this summer
campout
caesura
an ecstatic twist
from
the follicle
protest molecule
spawns
spurious rumors
in Oakland
only rent
a river
the burns
palpitate skin
in water
into bite-sized
bundles
tied ribbon
floating warm
the live-
long day

Oh, that's rich
said the boys in blue,
how do you think we measure theory
to full blown riot
thanks Mr. Richter
way to mock
the official stratagems
oh, what a formidable goddess
oh, what blue comedy
turning the screw
the mob is a mosaic of odors
this magical revival
is fertile and prolific
so as soon as
the internet pops
they start running
stage left

Gangway guys!

great Godmother, great
Cannibal Holocaust with headphones
those stupid engravings
you meditate upon
are for tourists and Greeks
how else to compute MDMA
but a bowl of Dandelions for dinner,
the tadpole burns on the blacktop
I'm headed for bed
I love you like a slow cooked meal,
like a tub-a-lard in a cul-de-sac
like two small animals
smiling in Japan

In nature
there are no negations
I'm eating nectar
clad in the skins
of wild beasts
stampeding through the vista
it's a long shot
over the mesa
the way I wake in the morning
with polished spear
one ear wet on my pillow

I am so sad and miss my leisure
what a waste of time
soaking in a hot spring can be,
I have this grammar
to bookmark my injuries
I'm sitting in a park
on a Sunday afternoon
sun-beams above me
like a lovely linen gown
I'm thinking about
what the ocean
might look like today
I don't recognize my name
when you say it
I've spent my summer
facing an expanse of water

Whoever invented the Cowboy Hat
gave himself permission
to not be cool
Jimmy Carter was a peanut farmer
Ed Leedskalnin
was literarily magnetic
Vernon Davis is crying
on Planet HULK,
holy fuckamole
that's cool

I knew a witch in Antioch, okay
I wrapped my druggy penis in a warm wet sock,
no way
it's not the party I thought it was going to be
it's not really a haunted house

Christos Anesti, Alithos Anesti
please don't call me Pap
I love Japanese food, I eat
Japanese as much as possible
it's important to me that people
see me enjoying Japanese food
as much as humanly possible
I'm not a Catholic boy
I never made the A team
nothing is as straightforward
or as simple
as time travel,
wet dreams

I sat in my father's dojo
talking a lot of marginal shit
I slept for 12 straight hours
and now I'm like the Muses,
if I was an animal
I'd be like the pioneers
grubstaked
enjoying the taste of blood

I've been late to supper
and suddenly there's a Seraphim on my arm
and I'm suddenly advocating Nintendo Power
I was right there with you
until you fed me all that Japanese candy
that dolphins rape is besides the point
my New Year's resolution:
stop reading the comments
emotions are not science
like the ignoble drone of a Canadian Goose
uprocking on linoleum, the coxcomb
of the cuckold instills a mounting sense of dread
my way or the highway BOB
I'm done making my kid's childhood magical

I miss $$$F, the clouds used to speak to me
I mean I could see language in the actual clouds
in the morning those runes hovering above my house
freebasing a thick cloud too, those portraits of clouds
changed the way I saw animals, commingling
the clouds falling from my mouth
there are always swimmers
under the bridge
the vast distances
bridging the stars
seemed to be sunshine stretched too thin, like
the Caldecott is a bottleneck and
love is a lonely weekend

It is a comfort
to sit in a straight-backed chair
and think
about the divinity
of numbers,
an iconoclast
is one
who destroys icons,
I've changed my mind
an iconoclast
affirms the embroidery
of the world,
there is a distinction
between veneration
and worship
I'm grateful for the ability
to weep
like the moon,
I have ruined the music
by sitting
in the back row

(Sunday Of Orthodoxy) March

There are no windows in the Presidio
only turrets to piss into
I'm compelled to light the candle
to peer into the clouds, little by little
this mechanical fastening
becomes a railway (to mention just one material)
I hear outer voices while playing the piano
a list of Saints learned by heart
St. Hilarion
St. Haralambos
no one who has not experienced these phenomena
can have any idea of the extent to which speech has
slowed down
obviously I'm lacking an inner voice

I may have eaten too much quiche
what if I only ate pickles?
a Double George Dickel please
she's no scream queen
she's QUOTA QUEEN
is it controversial
to say that
women don't shower as much as men
I'm addicted to this atmospheric river
again, who invented the cowboy hat
who's whistling Dixie
on the last train to Pittsburg

I was too young
for In Utero
haha
at 10AM the sun will be shining
and I'll be sweating,
what a lovely mist
we saw in Hawaii
the roads are winding
and I puke
but what a lovely
toad we found in the grass
the size of a football
I want to boot it
toward the carousel
the weight of its body
on a bright blue day
falling where it will

There is a house
that is intensely haunted
I can't tell whether this house
is splendor, foreign language
or pain
I sit in this house and think
if you drop a reptile from the clouds
you should probably have a map,
around every corner
is a mirror with a memory
it's winter
and sunlight is failing
I just have to wait
for these scenes to dissolve
hills rise and fall too
where do I find wonder
while soaking wet
remind me
what the swelling flower
and leaf discover
having you in mind
beyond waking

Quail

his skin
is water in a glass
like old flint
the lights
slammed weirdly
against him,
his name
none other than
potions and poison
now I remember
my good fortune

I was promised a jetpack
and boxes of candles
when Bob Grenier
said "I HATE SPEECH"
he meant technology
there can be no perception
without a perceiver,
speech is a selfie
not easily shrugged off
I'm content to be considerate
of others
multi-authored, the loner
is a liar

I am Apollo,
I am blind
I am not the sky
full of golden spice
I am earthquakes
the size of Christmas,
I was sent a postcard,
the whole sky awoke
a thin blue,
I was visited
by the sun
whose hairy arms
made me smile,
my eyes melted
stripped of nectar
I was sent a swan
blind and hapless
what a fragrant thing
well rounded, long-necked
goodbye sun
right to the edge
heavily to sleep

The ear is so troubled
below the earth
people here are stopping, just swimming

we looked down
a mass of chanting
a large pipe organ, to the left or to the right

I closed the door to my room
charting rock formations
the mechanics of the heart, is like a light projected

There's a pain in my ear drums
an oversized organ pipe
the reasons for singing, I am reading

the roar of the tiger
the calving of icebergs
this turbulent ardor, rectangles on the wall

I can't count to a thousand
as the avalanche approaches
I have been known to produce sounds, for hundreds of kilome-
ters

I am alone in a room reading
rereading actually about the animals fleeing
I am in awe of this collapsing, below the earth there are no rec-
tangles of light

events are often not observed
this loud cracking as the garland in snow
the supernatural nature of reading in a room, similar to seasick-
ness

staring in a crystal pretending it's a wind turbine
these two performances which are not my tradition
to be lifted out of a pool each morning, suggesting these odd sen-
sations

This pressure on my chest I attribute to sleep
I have closed the door on thresholds
revulsion has health risks, and may be loud to others

I know flux is a given
in this collapsing mountain
perhaps mammals can now find each other, by their holy names

large boats cannot approach a rectangular coordinate
similar to a humpback whale heading for other whales
light through a tsunami can feel vaguely odd or supernatural

I am in awe of thresholds
in particular, sleep disorders
I sit in my chair emitting two performances, heading for the herd

I keep walking on cold cement
I keep talking to people who are not here
I wasn't born at 20 Hz

the purr of felines
through solid ground
god is pure color in the presence of snow

Mysteriously snuffed out candles
the long blue fall of snow
reading the jargon, on a black wet day

the desk was the center
white, cinder, ivy-
the size of the landscape, the hound of white hell

there is also a beauty
near the edge of hearing
ghosts in the machine, "red, russet, brown"

GOD THE FATHER
FREAK-NIK
FOLLOWS SUIT
WHY BOTHER
BARGAINING
WITH THE
HARBINGER
HOLDING HIS
OWN ESSENCE
HOSTAGE, HIS
RENTS ROTTEN
HIS KINGDOM
HAS NO END